An Everyday Adventure Series
by Moji Taiwo

Grandma & her Munchkins

Gardening with Grandma

Illustrations by Cristiana Tercero

For my precious Munchkins: Ezra, Caxton, and Amos.
Spending time with you boys brings me vitality and endless joy.

Copyright © Moji Taiwo

All rights reserved. No part of this book may be reproduced by any mechanical, photographic, or electronic process or in the form of phonographic recording; nor may it be stored in a retrieval system, transmitted, or otherwise copied for public or private use without the prior written permission of the author at mojitaiwo1@gmail.com.
ISBN (paperback): 978-1-7782838-5-7 / ISBN (Ebook): 978-1-7751235-5-2 / ISBN (IngramSpark): 978-1-7782838-1-9

Moji Taiwo
www.mojitaiwo.com

In the Springtime, when the weather starts to warm up and the rain came, we learnt how to plant seeds and grow vegetables from grandma.

Grandma collected rainwater in her garden barrel.
She says the rain is good for growing her garden and
we learnt to save water when we collected the rain.

We put small seeds of carrots,
and peas,
and spinach
and sunflowers
in tiny cups with soil and a little bit of water.

We put the cups inside a mini green house inside Grandma's kitchen.
We put it by the window so that it can get some sunlight.

We also learnt that plants need water and sunlight to grow.

After the snow melts and it's not freezing outside anymore,
We put our little plants into the ground, in grandma's garden to grow.

We planted in the sunshine area and gave them water from grandma's rain barrel everyday.

Now you know that plants need sunshine and water to grow!

This was one of our favorite activities when we got water from the barrel in a water canteen...

And we watched the plants grow taller and bigger throughout the summer.

Look at our carrots! We pulled out some and ate them, they tasted yummy.

But Baby Munchkin liked the peas the most.

We ate lots of vegetables because Grandma said it will help us grow taller and healthy.

Look at the sunflowers, they have grown taller than us.
"Yay! the sunflowers are *'ginormous'*,
reaching all the way to the sky!"; said Junior Munchkin.

Fall season was the end of the gardening season for grandma.

We helped her to harvest all the vegetables and herbs and cleaned up the garden.

The weather got cold in the fall, and all the leaves turned to rainbow colours.

What's your favourite vegetable to eat?

www.ingramcontent.com/pod-product-compliance
Lightning Source LLC
Chambersburg PA
CBHW040023130526
44590CB00036B/75